Rush to the Bus

Written by Suzy Senior

Illustrated by Sian James

Collins

Liz and Josh rush to the bus.

3

Liz will get tickets.

5

But the cash is not in her pocket!

Josh thinks it is by the bin.

Yes. This is it.

Then off they go.

13

/sh/

15

 After reading

Letters and Sounds: Phase 3

Word count: 40

Focus phonemes: /j/ /w/ /y/ /z/ /qu/ /sh/ /th/ /ng/ /nk/

Common exception words: and, to, the, her, by, they, you

Curriculum links: Understanding the world; Personal, social and emotional development

Early learning goals: Reading: read and understand simple sentences; use phonic knowledge to decode regular words and read them aloud accurately; read some common irregular words

Developing fluency

- Your child may enjoy hearing you read the book.
- Take turns to read a page. Check your child notices the exclamation marks and reads these sentences with extra emphasis.

Phonic practice

- Ask your child to reread pages 4 and 5, then identify the words where two letters make one sound: **will** (*ll*), **tickets** (*ck*), **Hang** (*ng*).
- Repeat for page 8: **Josh** (*sh*), **thinks** (*th, nk*). Your child might also notice the single sound made by "th" in **the**.
- Look at the "I spy sounds" pages (14 and 15) together. Tell your child you are going to look for words containing the sounds /y/ and /sh/. Point to the yacht and say "yacht", emphasising the /y/ sound. Point to the shark and say "shark", emphasising the /sh/ sound. Challenge your child to find more words containing these sounds. (e.g. *yawn, yoyo, yoghurt*; *shopping, shoes, shirt, shampoo*)

Extending vocabulary

- Talk to your child about the meaning of **tickets**. What other tickets can they think of? (e.g. *theatre, car park, fairground*)
- Reread page 5 and talk about the meaning of **Hang on**. Can your child think of another meaning for **Hang on**? (e.g. *hold tight*) When might someone shout "Hang on!" and mean "hold tight"? (e.g. *when on a swing or roundabout*)